LET'S TALK
ABOUT THE
SABBATH

Dorothy K. Kripke

Illustrated by Stacy Crossland
& Joy Nelkin Weider

Alef Design Group

Library of Congress Catalonging-in-Publication Data

Kripke, Dorothy Karp.

Let's talk about the Sabbath / Dorothy K. Kripke; illustrated by Stacy Crossland & Joy Nelkin Weider.

p.   c.m.

Summary: Explains the customs which make the Jewish sabbath a holy and joyful day.

ISBN 1-881283-18-6

1. Sabbath—Juvenile Literature. [1. Sabbath. 2. Judaism—Customs and practices.] I. Crossland, Stacy, ill. II. Weider, Joy Nelkin, ill. III. Title.

BM685.K757 1999

296.4'1—dc21   98-56053

CIP

AC

ISBN# 1-881283-18-6
Copyright © 1999 Dorothy K. Kripke
Illustrations and Cover art copyright © 1999 Joy Nelkin Weider
Illustrations copyright © 1999 Stacy Crossland
Published by Alef Design Group

Alef Design Group • 4423 Fruitland Avenue, Los Angeles, Ca 90058
(800) 845–0662 • (323) 582-1200 • (323) 585–0327 fax
www.alefdesign.com
MANUFACTURED IN THE UNITED STATES OF AMERICA

In Memory of

Goldie and Max Karp

who hallowed the Sabbath

and "called it a delight"

and for their great-grandchildren

Gil and Tamar Stern

who are learning to delight

in the SABBATH

Letter to the Young Reader

Dear Reader,

Have you ever found secret treasure? You really can! Where? In "make-believe" stories! Not gold, or silver, or jewels, but something even more precious—ideas!

"Make-believe" stories often tell us important things. Sometimes, the important ideas, like secret treasure, are hidden, and we must hunt to find them. Here are two such stories. Can you find the ideas in them?

Somewhere (no one knows exactly where, because it's only "make-believe"), there is a river called the Sambatyon. The Sambatyon whirls and swirls and churns and roars. For six days. On the seventh day of each week it stops. It is quiet and peaceful. On the Sabbath, it rests.

Now, the second story. The Emperor of Rome once asked a Rabbi, "What makes your Sabbath food smell so good? Do you flavor it with a special spice? What is this spice?"

"You are right," answered the Rabbi. "We do have a very special spice. It is—the Sabbath!"

"In that case," beamed the Emperor, "just give me a little of your spice. Then my food, too, will be wonderfully fragrant and delicious."

"Not so," replied the Rabbi. "This precious spice works automatically—but only for those who observe the Sabbath—and treasure it."

Dorothy K. Kripke

Contents

CHAPTER 1
Queen of the Days — The Sabbath

The Sabbath comes to bless the week,
One day in every seven,
To bless us with its holiness,
A tiny taste of heaven.

IF YOU WERE EXPECTING A QUEEN TO VISIT in your home, what would you do? You would want your home to sparkle and glisten. You would dress in your best clothes. You would prepare the best possible foods and goodies. You would want to be completely free from your usual work and chores, so that you could spend all your time with your guest. You would invite friends to come and enjoy your guest and your treats with you.

This is exactly how our people have always felt about the Sabbath. The best of everything is saved for this day. The usual work of the week is set aside, for this is a day of peace and joy, a day of refreshment and rest.

Shabbat, the Sabbath, is a very special day for Jewish people. So special, indeed, that it is called the Holy Sabbath. So beloved is the Sabbath that it is called the Bride. So honored is the day that it is called Sabbath, the Queen.

Why do we rest on the Sabbath? The Bible tells us that God worked for six days to make the world. Then, on the seventh day, the Sabbath, He stopped working and rested. And He wants people to rest too. This is so important that we are even told about the Sabbath in the Ten Commandments: "Remember the Sabbath Day and keep it holy."

Shabbat reminds us of something else too. It reminds us that we were freed from the slavery of Egypt. Slaves cannot rest when they wish. Free people can. Free people can work hard all week and do the important work of the world. Then they can spend a whole day just paying attention to something that is in each of us, a little bit of God.

For thousands of years, it was this day of rest that refreshed all Jews, wherever they lived. In their lively imagination, the Sabbath was a little, precious taste of heaven here on earth.

CHAPTER 2
We Prepare for a Guest

Hurry, hurry, hurry,
There's work that must be done!
For all must be in readiness
Ere Sabbath has begun.

IT IS FRIDAY, AND WE ARE EXPECTING A VERY important guest. Mother and her helpers are busy making the house shine and sparkle. The brasses gleam; the silver glistens. In a vase, fresh flowers, white and yellow and pale orange, nestle among green leaves and softly whisper a warm welcome. Dad too does everything he can to have everything ready for Shabbat.

From stove and oven and pantry shelves, wonderful smells blend and fill the house with a tempting fragrance. Our mouths water, and we can hardly wait to taste.

During the week, choice treats have been set aside and saved to enjoy with the guest. If on Thursday, Mother has baked crisp, crunchy cookies, the family gets only a taste. They are being saved—to eat on Shabbat.

 The table is set with care. The candles, standing proudly in their polished holders, are ready to be lit. The tray of hallah, the braided, golden Sabbath bread, is covered with a decorated hallah cloth. The sparkling wine bottle and the gleaming Kiddush cup, too, are ready. Everything is ready for the guest.

Who is this very important guest? It is the
Sabbath, the Holy Sabbath, Queen of the Days,
beloved of the Jew.

CHAPTER 3
Candles and Wine

The sun hangs low and twilight falls.
The work of the day is done.
Our guest is here. In peace and joy
The Sabbath has begun.

THE SUN SINKS LOW IN THE WESTERN SKY.
The hustle and the bustle of the day are done. The
hurry and the scurry of the week are gone. All is
calm. A sense of peace fills both home and heart.
The Sabbath candles are lit.

We light the candles with a prayer: "We thank
You, O Lord our God, King-of-the-Universe, for
making us holy by Your commandments, and for
commanding us to kindle the Sabbath lights." And

in our hearts, we add a silent prayer that God will bless our families and friends with life and health and joy—and all the world with peace.

Later, as the family sits down to dinner, everyone raises the Kiddush cup filled with wine, and chants the Kiddush. In the old and beautiful words of the Kiddush, we thank God for having given us, in love, this precious day of  rest and delight. This is a day, the Kiddush tells us, to remind us that God rested on the seventh day from all the work of Creation, of making the world. And it is to remind us, too, that God freed us from the slavery of Egypt. We are free people, and are free to rest.

This loving gift, this holy day of peace and rest and joy, makes us holy too.

CHAPTER 4
Sabbath Angels

Escorted by angels, angels of peace,
Comes Sabbath, the Queen, the Bride.
And Israel, her bridegroom, stands
Devoted at her side.

ON SABBATH EVE, THE SYNAGOGUE TOO has a feeling of peace and rest and joy. There are special Sabbath prayers. Early in the service, there is an especially beautiful song-poem in which the Jewish people, welcoming the Sabbath, is pictured as a bridegroom going forth to meet his bride.

O Israel come, come greet your bride;
Come, welcome the Sabbath at eventide.

So real is the feeling of peace, that we even imagine angels of peace about us on the Sabbath. So, in the Synagogue or at home, we sing a song of welcome to these "make-believe" angels.

Welcome in peace, O angels who serve,
Messengers from above, from God,
the King Who rules all kings,
Whom we revere and love.

Come, now, in peace, O angels of peace…

Bless me with peace, O angels of peace…

Farewell and peace, O angels of peace,
Messengers from above, from God,
the King Who rules all kings,
Whom we revere and love.

Long ago, our people, who liked to let their imaginations play, imagined that all Jews, when they went home from the Synagogue on Sabbath eve, were accompanied by two Sabbath angels, one good, one bad. If everything at home was peaceful

 and ready for the Sabbath, the good angel would say, "So be it in the week to come." And the bad angel, even though he didn't really want to, would be forced to answer, "Amen." But if the home was not ready and not peaceful, the bad angel would say, "So be it in the week to come." And the good angel, against his will and very sad, was forced to whisper, "Amen."

Now we know that angels are only a kind of poetry, a lovely "make-believe." But what our people were really saying, in both song and story, is that they had a strong feeling of Sabbath peace. And we can have it too.

CHAPTER 5
Study and Prayer

The Torah and the Haftarah
We chant and study too.
For study is a kind of prayer
That's precious to a Jew.

SABBATH MORNING IS ESPECIALLY A TIME FOR Synagogue services. At the service there are prayers added for Shabbat. But perhaps the most important part of all is the reading, really a chanting, from the Torah, the first five books of the Bible.

It was the reading of the Torah that started the whole idea of the Synagogue. The people wanted to know what the Torah says, so that they might know God's will and do it. So they got together, and each week they read the portion of the Torah that followed the portion they had read the week before. So important was study of Torah to our people that it became a kind of prayer and a part of prayer. And it still is.

This reading of the Torah week after week and year after year does important things for the Jewish people. Each Sabbath we read the same part of the Torah that other Jews are reading all over the world, wherever Jews live. This makes us feel that we belong to each other. And because we read now what our people have read for hundreds and hundreds of years and will read hundreds of years from now, we belong to the Jews of the past and to those who will live in time that is to come. And they belong to us!

Reading a definite Torah Portion each week does another interesting thing. Each Torah Portion has a name. For example, the Torah Portion that tells the story of Noah and the flood is called "Portion Noah." Have you ever stopped to think that other people have names or numbers for the days, the months, and the years, but none for the weeks? But we do! Because we read the Torah week after week, we have names for the week too. We call the week by the name of the Torah Portion. So, for example, the week that "Portion Noah" is read in the Synagogue is called by that name.

 On Shabbat morning, and on holidays too, after the chanting of the Torah there is another chanted reading, the Haftarah. This is a passage taken from another part of the Bible.

Both the Torah Portion and the Haftarah are a kind of study. And study is a very important part of Jewish prayer. So we see that Shabbat is not only a day of rest and joy; it is also a day of prayer and study.

CHAPTER 6
We Feel Like Royalty

Gone the labors of the week
And all unpleasant things.
For when the Sabbath comes at last,
All Jews are queens and kings.

THE SABBATH MORNING SERVICE IS OVER. We are at home again and ready for dinner. Often there are guests. Shabbat gives us a company feeling, so that we ourselves seem to be guests in our own home. And dinner is a company meal.

Dinner starts with a short Kiddush, again chanted over a cup of wine. The food is delicious. And the leisurely mood, the feeling that no one is in a great hurry, makes the food seem even more tasty. At the table, some families sing Sabbath hymns. These tell of the peace and the joy of the day. They tell, too, of God's wondrous works and of the many things God does for us. This singing adds a wonderful flavor to the food. Dinner ends with the Grace after Meals, in which we thank God for the good world we live in.

Forgotten are the work and the worries of the week. It is as though they are locked away in an attic trunk. Father feels like a king. Mother feels like a queen. The Sabbath spirit makes the simplest home, as though by a kind of magic, seem like a palace.

After dinner, like royalty, we relax. Some people even take a short nap. Perhaps we visit friends. Or they visit us. We drink tea or lemonade together. We munch crisp cookies and other treats. And there are treats for the mind too. We read and we study.

For the Sabbath is not a day for working or doing; it is a day for thinking and feeling. It is a day for remembering that there is a  little of God in each of us. All this is what the Rabbis of old meant when they said that on the Sabbath the Jew had an "extra soul." They meant that on the Sabbath the Jew had a special feeling of peace and joy and holiness.

In times past, our people kept the Sabbath Day, and it gave them this wonderful feeling. Nowadays, not every Jewish family is fortunate enough to be able to keep the day in this lovely way. But the more we "Remember the Sabbath Day and keep it holy," the more we enjoy its rich rewards.

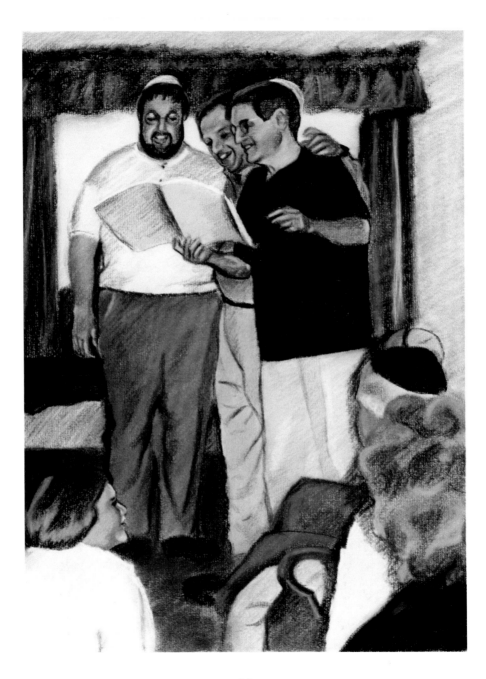

CHAPTER 7
Oneg Shabbat— & Sabbath Joy

Sabbath joy
And Sabbath pleasure
Come this day
In special measure.

THE SABBATH IS A DAY OF DELIGHT, A DAY
OF JOY.

Why, then, are there so many "Sabbath don'ts"?
We are told not to do any work or chores on the
Sabbath that can be done at another time—or left
undone. But all these "don'ts" are really to make
possible the important "Sabbath do." The
important "do" is to remember our own holiness,

to pay attention to the little bit of God in each of us.

How do we do this? We do this by keeping the Sabbath as a day of rest and peace and joy. To the Jew, who found joy in so many things, an important part of joy was study.

So, in the past, in order to have *Oneg Shabbat*, Sabbath Joy, Jews would go to the Synagogue. There, in the late afternoon, they would gather to study. They would sing Sabbath songs, sometimes melodies without words. They would have a "Third Feast." This was a light, but lovely, Sabbath supper that seemed to have a separate Sabbath flavor. The study, the

singing, the food, all this was *Oneg Shabbat*, Sabbath Joy, joy for the body and joy for the spirit.

In our own times, a great Hebrew poet living in the Land of Israel used to invite friends to *Oneg Shabbat* gatherings. The idea spread. In homes or Synagogues, Jews gathered for study or discussion, for singing and dancing and refreshments. They enjoyed the "get-together" and called it an *Oneg Shabbat*.

Soon it became a popular idea not only in the Land of Israel but in America and other countries, too. *Oneg Shabbat*, Sabbath Joy, is an old Jewish idea made new.

CHAPTER 8
Havdalah—
Farewell to a Holy Day

With wine and spice and candle,
The Sabbath Day departs.
And well we know, as we see her go,
The working week now starts.

AS THE SUN SETS, THE DAYLIGHT SLIPS QUIETLY away. Stars twinkle in the darkening sky. Shabbat, our guest, is ready to leave. Sorry as we are to see her go, we know that we must bid her farewell.

Just as we greeted the Sabbath with blessings, with candlelight, wine, and song, so, too, do we take our leave of her. We have Havdalah, a ceremony that separates the holy day from the ordinary weekday.

In this leave-taking ceremony, we light the colorful, braided Havdalah candle, with its several wicks, and hands it to a child to hold high. Now we raise our wine goblets and chant the blessing. Holding the Havdalah spice box, we chant a blessing as we take a whiff of its fragrance. We pass it around for the rest of the family to enjoy. Then, as we watch the flame that rises from the braided candle, we thank God for light. We chants our praise of God, Who separates light from darkness and the Holy Sabbath from the six working days. Now at last we sip the wine. The holy day is over; a new week has begun.

Now, too, there are special songs. In one song we wish each other a happy week. In another we hope for the speedy coming of the time when this will be a better world.

When guests are ready to leave, we "see them to the door." This is a way of saying we are sorry to see them go. We want to spend these last few moments with them before we say "good-bye." Just so, the Havdalah  ceremony bids farewell to the Holy Sabbath and escorts her on her way. With feelings of hope it greets the new working week and welcomes it. And between the two, Havdalah stands as a clear mark of separation.

CHAPTER 9
Shabbat Blesses Our Celebrations

As growing plants turn toward the sun
And gain strength from its rays,
So Jews turn toward Shabbat to find
True blessing in the days.

FOR MANY, MANY HUNDREDS OF YEARS,
the week, in the Jewish home, turned toward the
Sabbath. And in many Jewish homes, it still does.
On Wednesday, Thursday, and Friday, thoughts
turn toward the Shabbat that is coming. The house
and clothes must be made ready. Treats are saved
and favorite foods are prepared. On Sunday,
Monday, Tuesday, the home still feels the glow and

the magic of the Sabbath that has passed. The whole week seems to revolve around the Sabbath.

In something of the same way, the great moments in the life of the Jew, the most important occasions, seem to turn toward the Sabbath.

When a baby is born, a prayer is said in the Synagogue at the Torah reading, usually on the Sabbath, for the health of mother and child. And if the new baby is a girl, she is given her name at the Torah reading.

A boy is usually named at a ceremony called *Brit Milah* that is only rarely held in the Synagogue. Usually it is held in the hospital where the new baby was born, or in the home.

Nowadays a baby girl is also given her name at a ceremony called *Simhat Bat* (joy in our daughter). This a new ceremony created to be like the joy parents have at the *Brit Milah* for a boy baby. It is usually held at home.

On reaching the age of thirteen, a boy becomes a bar mitzvah (and in many synagogues a girl becomes a bat mitzvah), again at the Torah reading, usually on Shabbat. Religiously, they now have the privileges and responsibilities of grown-ups.

Before a wedding, the bridegroom is called to the Torah reading, usually on the Sabbath. In many Synagogues the bride joins her bridegroom at the Torah. This is a happy occasion for the families of bridegroom and bride. Often the groom's family invites the entire congregation to share its happiness by staying for Kiddush, right after services. Cake and wine are served, sometimes a luncheon too, in honor of the occasion and, at the same time, in honor of the Sabbath.

It is at the Torah reading, too, that special prayers are said for the sick. We pray that God will bless them and bring them back to health. Sometimes there are people who have escaped a great danger, like flood or serious accident. They want to thank God. For this prayer, too, they are "called to the Torah."

Now, we see that these important points in the life of a Jew are connected with the Torah reading. Now the Torah is read on Mondays and Thursdays, as well as on holidays and Shabbat. So all life's "great moments" can be celebrated in the Synagogue at these other times, too. And sometimes they are. But, somehow, unless there is a definite reason for choosing another time, we choose Shabbat.

The Jew seems to turn to Shabbat as growing plants turn toward the sun. As plants gain strength from the sun, so the spirit of the Jew gains strength from the Sabbath.

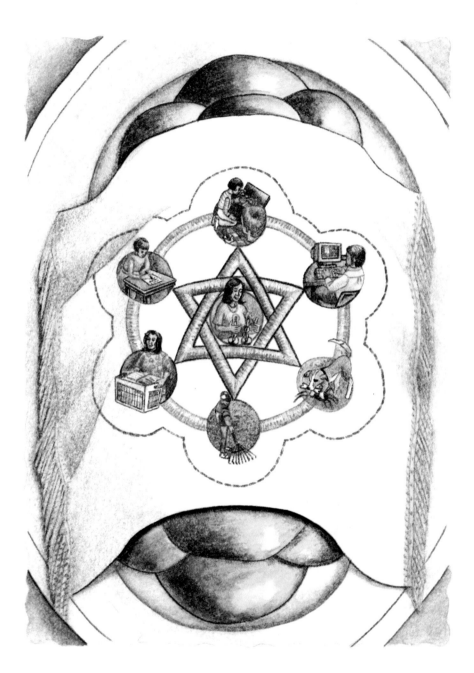

44

CHAPTER 10
About Work and Rest—
A New Idea

We must work that we may live;
But we must also rest
To feel that in ourselves we have
A spark of holiness.

JUDAISM TEACHES THAT WORK IS GOOD.
Work is necessary so that people will have food and
clothing and homes and many other things, even
"fun things." And Judaism teaches that rest is
good. Rest is necessary so that we may truly enjoy
all the things we work for. And when we rest, we
are even more able to feel the holiness that is in us.

In olden times there were some people who never worked, and there were others who always worked. They worked day after day, week after week, year after year. Like work animals, they never rested.

But Judaism had a different idea. In the Ten Commandments, the fourth one tells us:

"Remember the Sabbath Day and keep it holy. Six days you shall labor and do all your work, but the seventh day is a Sabbath of the Lord your God: you shall not do any work...."

The Jew was taught that it is good to work. It is important to do the work of the world. And it is good to rest, to remember that we are not just animals or machines, to remember that there is a little of God in each of us.

So, on the seventh day, on Shabbat, the Jew rested. This was a new idea in the world. The Greeks and the Romans thought it very strange. Their workers never had a day of rest. The Jews, they said, were a lazy people.

In time, however, when the Christian religion arose it liked the Jewish idea of rest. So it continued the Jewish idea. But, in order to be different, and for other reasons too, it changed the day from the seventh to the first, from Saturday to Sunday. Later, when the Muslim religion grew, it too borrowed the Jewish idea, but changed the day. The sixth day, Friday, became the Muslim day of rest. So this Jewish idea, strange at first, was eventually used in a large part of the world.

When we "Remember the Sabbath day and keep it holy," we remember that we are holy too.

CHAPTER 11
The Sabbath Has Kept the Jewish People

Relaxed, refreshed, our strength renewed,
Our sense of worth restored,
All Jews, on Sabbath, came alive;
It was the week's reward.

FOR ABOUT TWO THOUSAND YEARS
the Jewish people has been scattered all over the
world. Today we are comfortable in most, though
not all, of the countries where we live. In many
ways, we live as most other people do. But in the
past it was quite different. In most of the countries
where Jews lived, they were considered strangers.
People were afraid of strangers. They did not like
strangers.

49

So there were many things Jews were not allowed to do. They could not go to schools, except Jewish ones. They could not choose where they would live. They all had to live in the same part of the city, a ghetto, the worst and poorest part. They could not choose how they would earn a living. They had to do the work that no one else wanted to do. If something bad happened, like sickness or plague, the easiest ones to blame were these "strangers," the Jews. If there was war, no matter how ridiculous the charge, the Jews were blamed. Jews were often attacked by the very people among whom they lived. They lived in misery and fear.

For six days of the week. But not so on the seventh! For the seventh day was Shabbat. And Shabbat had a kind of magic for Jews. The misery of the week was gone. Dressed in their best clothes, their homes shining, their tables laden with the best foods they could afford, Jews were kings and queens. Sabbath rest and Sabbath joy gave them a sense of peace, of self-respect, of dignity. It was as though they had found a well of living water that cleansed them of all the misery of the week that was past. Refreshed, they now had strength and courage to face the week that was to come. Six days they toiled and struggled; but on Shabbat Jews really lived.

They knew, too, that all over the world, Jews were keeping the Sabbath as they were. They were reading the same Torah Portion; they were saying the same prayers; they were feeling the same Sabbath peace. They felt they belonged to all the others and they to them. And Abraham, to whom God promised so much, and wise Moses, and David, the brave poet-king, and all the Jews of the past and all the Jews who would live in time to come, these, too, were his people, his "family." However poor they were, the Sabbath made them

understand that in the things that really mattered, they were very rich indeed.

All this was what a great Hebrew writer meant when he said, "More than the Jewish people has kept the Sabbath, the Sabbath has kept the Jewish people."

CHAPTER 12
It's Up to Us

The plant we treat with tender care
Will give us joy and pleasure;
The Sabbath, if we keep the day,
Can yield us life's best treasure.

SUPPOSE SOMEONE GAVE YOU A PLANT,
a bulb nursed into a young plant in a pretty green
pot, and told you that if you took care of it, it would
blossom. If you forgot to water it and care for it, it
would wither before you could enjoy its blooms.
But if you gave it the right amount of sun and
water and plant food, if you cared for it properly,
the leaves would grow firm and green and healthy.
After a while, buds would appear. Soon the buds
would open and blossom into a lovely hyacinth,

white and lavender or even pink. Its delicate color and rich perfume would give you pleasure.

So it is with the Sabbath. The Jew who forgets to keep it properly, who does not care for it, forfeits its strength and beauty. But the Jew who remembers that it is God's loving gift, who keeps it with love and care, shares its beauty, its peace, its joy, its rich rewards. Do you remember the story of the Rabbi and the Emperor? Isn't this really what the Rabbi told the Emperor?

In Israel, stores and offices are closed on the Sabbath. But in other countries it may not be so easy to observe the Sabbath. This is why your Sabbath may be different. Family members who work cannot so easily stay home from the office, the store, or work. But they can still light the Sabbath candles, chant Kiddush, have a special dinner, and say the Grace after Meals. They can still do some of the other Sabbath things. If they really think of it, the family can do on weekdays all the weekday things, like shopping and laundry. They can save Shabbat for Synagogue and rest and other Sabbath things. The home can still be prepared for Shabbat, the home sparkling, the meals special. There can still be the Sabbath feeling. Shabbat can still be a special day, a day of peace and prayer and joy.

For some reason we may not be able to give our hyacinth plant its plant food. But we still give it sun and water. And its beauty and fragrance will still give us pleasure. Perhaps we cannot keep the Sabbath exactly as it was kept in the past, but there are many things we can do.

We can keep it as a day to remember the little bit of God in each of us. In many ways, we can "Remember the Sabbath Day and keep it holy."

Yah Ribbon— Master of the World
A Sabbath Hymn

Master of the world
And all that it contains,
Almighty God, the King of kings,
Who through all ages reigns,
Your wondrous works call forth my thanks
In prayers and in refrains.
Your wondrous works call forth my thanks
In prayers and in refrains.

By day, and in the night,
O God, I sing Your praise.
To You, Who made all living things,
My voice, in thanks, I raise.
O You, Who made both bird and beast,
I bless You all my days.
O You, Who made both bird and beast,
I bless You all my days.

Dorothy K. Kripke was born in upstate New York and educated in New York City public schools. She holds a B.A. degree from Hunter College and an M.A. in English from Columbia University, as well as a B.H.L. (Bachelor of Hebrew Literature) from the Jewish Theological Seminary of America.

In 1937, after teaching English briefly in a New York High School, she married Rabbi Myer S. Kripke, whose career took her to Wisconsin, Long Island, Connecticut, and, finally, to Omaha, Nebraska. In each of these places she taught Hebrew and Judaism to children and adults.

An unusually and creative teacher, Dorothy began writing little rhymes about Judaism and about life, which she recited or "sang" for her own children. Some of these reached book form.

When she complained to her husband that there were no good books about God for children, he replied, "Then write one." Mrs. Kripke did so—the best-seller *Let's Talk About God* (Behrman House)—and went on to write and have published more books, both in the *Let's Talk* series and with other titles. Her publication list includes: *Let's Talk About Right and Wrong, Let's Talk About Judaism* and *God and the Story of Judaism* with Meyer Levin (Behrman House); *Let's Talk About Loving* with Rabbi Myer S. Kripke and *Let's Talk About Being Jewish* (KTAV); *Rhymes to Play* and *Rhymes to Pray* (Bloch Publishing); *Debbie in Dreamland* (National Women's League); and *Let's Talk About the Jewish Holidays* (Jonathan David).

Rabbi and Mrs. Kripke still live in Omaha. Their children and two grandchildren all live in the East.

Other titles from Alef Design Group
(& Torah Aura Productions

MIDDLE READERS—8-11 YEARS OLD

Sing Time
Bruce H. Siegel

A ten-year-old discovers in half an hour how a single teacher, a Cantor, can impact his life. This Cantor doesn't just sing songs, he shares the value of a single moment in time, and how music is the "calendar" of Jewish life. Cantor Jacobs steers our hero down a path he might never have taken otherwise, all because his dad decided that Jerry-the-Jerk (his older brother, Gerald) should have a bar mitzvah.

Softcover • Middle Reader • Jewish Connections
ISBN # 1-881283-14-3 • $5.95

The Grey Striped Shirt
Jacqueline Jules

Frannie is looking for Grandma's purple hat with the feather. By accident she discovers a grey striped shirt with a yellow star hidden in the back of the closet. As she begins asking her grandparents questions, they begin to unfold the story of their Holocaust experience. This novel for middle readers gently reveals the truths about the Holocaust without reducing it to a horror show.

Softcover • Middle Reader • Holocaust • ISBN #1-881283-21-6 • $8.50

Tanta Teva & the Magic Booth
Joel Lurie Grishaver

It all started when Marc (with a "C") Zeiger ran away one night to get his parents to buy him a Virtual Reality hook-up (it's a long story). In the dark, lost in a part of the woods which couldn't possibly exist, he encounters Tanta Teva, a cleaning lady who is busy scrubbing graffiti off rocks in the forest. Together they visit young Joshua, David and Hillel. When Marc returns home, no one really believes the stories of where he'd been and who he'd met!

Softcover • Middle Reader • Fantasy • ISBN #1-881283-00-3 • $5.95

Dear Hope... Love, Grandma
Hilda Abramson Hurwitz & Hope R. Wasburn, Edited by Mara H. Wasburn

Eight-year-old Hope had a school project to become the summer pen pal of a senior citizen. When her assigned pen pal failed to write back, her mother suggested she write to her grandmother. A two-year correspondence resulted. This book is a collection of letters in which Grandma reveals the stories of her childhood, the difficulties growing up in turn-of-the-century St. Louis, and some wonderful and joyous insights about human hearts.

Hardcover • Middle Reader • Autobiography •
ISBN #1-881283-03-8 • $13.95

Two Cents & a Milk Bottle
Lee Chai'ah Batterman

This outstanding juvenile novel, set in 1937, follows twelve-year-old Leely Dorman as she faces a new neighborhood, a new school and new friends. Over the course of the novel, Leely becomes a friend, an entrepreneur, and the first girl in the neighborhood to study to become a bat mitzvah. A wonderful ending ties in themes of the Hanukkah holiday.

Hardcover • Middle Reader • American Jewish History, Jewish Life •
1-881283-17-8 • $15.95

PICTURE BOOK

A Sense of Shabbat
Faige Kobre

In the sensuous photographs and simple text that make up this picture book, the taste, feel, sound, look and touch of the Jewish Sabbath all come alive. The Sabbath presented here is at once holy and wondrous, comfortable and familiar.

Hardcover • Picture Book • Sabbath
ISBN #0-933873-44-1 • $11.95

FOR FAMILIES

Mark Stark's Amazing Jewish Cookbook
Written and Illustrated by Mark Stark

This cookbook is a collection of secret family recipes and a celebration of Jewish cooking. Everything is ready for even the most beginning cook—hand-drawn recipes show the ingredients, the tools needed, and the steps used to make them. Recipes are listed by holiday, with a description of the holiday's celebration. All recipes are coded for adherence to kashrut, the religious and dietary laws of the Jewish people. For those who want to discover the fun of creative Jewish cooking, this book is a must.

Softcover • Family • Cooking/Jewish Life • ISBN #1-881283-19-4 • $26.50

Eight Nights, Eight Lights
Rabbi Kerry M. Olitzky

Courage. Gratitude. Sharing. Knowledge. Service. Understanding. Love. Hope. Eight nights. Eight lights. Eight family values. In this joyous and reflective work, Rabbi Kerry M. Olitzky provides families with a way of letting their Hanukkah celebrations affirm not only their Jewish identity, but the very Jewish values they wish to transmit to their children.

Softcover • Family/Hanukkah • ISBN #1-881283-09-7 • $8.95

ORDER BOOKS VIA
THE TORAH AURA PRODUCTIONS WEBSITE
AT WWW.TORAHAURA.COM
OR CALL ALEF DESIGN GROUP AT
(800) 845-0662 OR (323) 582-1200